GET ...
TO ...

LIVING AN OSCAR-WORTHY LIFE

DORIAN ALEXIS SANTIAGO

PUBLISHED BY TEAR PUBLISHING

TABLE OF CONTENTS

PRE-PRODUCTION

I am not even sure why I wrote this introduction and it really isn't a formal introduction but if you are like me, you are probably going to skip it. It is quite all right. I understand. Introductions are not normally filled with useful information, so, if you are this person, Production is waiting.

For those of you continuing to read and those of you who have come back (continuing readers – you will understand soon enough), I assure you this introduction will be both entertaining and insightful. It will be memorable and quotable. It will be moving and poignant. Oh, and spoiler alert...

You will know the meaning of life by the end of this book.
(SO TAKE NOTES)

LIFE is ACTING. ACTING is LIFE; not in the sense it is the greatest thing ever but rather that they are one in the same. The greatest acting is invisible; there is no distinction between an actor acting and a person being. Since this is the case, we should then realize the principles of great acting lend themselves to great living.

You want to get your act together. I am glad you purchased, borrowed, or stole this book. If you stole the book, just make sure after you become extremely successful, you repay the person you stole it from. I'm sure they will appreciate it.

First, I want you to know this book was created by using a traditional recipe of procrastination, failure, frustration, motherly criticism, appreciation for humanity, dedication to my passion, and the love of life and my craft. It is the result of a mid-life calling.

This book is for everyone; it is the culmination of knowledge that I've secured through my lifetime. It is a guide to creating a life that is Oscar-worthy. I use this term to define my own life, and I'd like to explain what it means in relation to living (ACTORS BE PATIENT). The reason an actor wins an Oscar is because they had an outstanding performance in a film. Our lives are films. We have an audience to them. Our audience will cheer with us, cry with us, criticize us, want more, and sometimes even stop watching. Our audience is our family, friends, teachers, and even some strangers at certain points in our lives.

The purpose of this book is to educate not motivate. If you are reading this book, you are already motivated. The problem doesn't lie in you wanting change, the problem lies is the how to change and for most people they want the easiest route.

It is a well-known fact that electricity travels in the path of least resistance. Well, aren't we just a bundle of electric organisms firing off simultaneously? We send an electric shock to our hearts to get it beating again. We use electronic stimuli to repair and rehabilitate muscles. We connect electrodes to our heads to see our brain activity. We are one big electric organism, so it makes sense we too will travel the path of least resistance.

Here it is. This book will be a revelation to some, a reminder to others, and an enigma to a few. I would say everything in this book you already know, but to know and not do, is the same as not knowing. With a little bit of analysis, I have found these ideas and beliefs make my life less stressful, less complicated, and less mundane while also making it more peaceful, more successful, and more meaningful. This is a how-to guide for simplifying your life, which if done properly will bring insurmountable success.

There are a couple of things you need. You won't find them lying around the house. You may have to seek them out, but once you have them, everything else is a breeze. Don't let the list discourage you. Some people will never find these things, some people have and don't know how to use them, and others find them early in life and utilize them to the best of their ability. Here they are in no particular order:

-Commitment
Even the path of least resistance still has resistance, so you'll have to make up your mind to do what it takes and do it.

-Faith
Unsuccessful people won't believe something until they see it. Successful people see things because they believe it. I'll show you it works, but it is much better going into this with a positive mind frame.

-Open Mind

Most of us have already been programmed or conditioned with certain beliefs. Realize if that set of beliefs worked for you, you would not be reading this book. Your life would already be Oscar-worthy.

Once you have these things, you are ready to continue. Don't read any further if you don't have them. It would be a waste of your time. That's right, I said it. You can stop reading my book if you don't truly have the three things needed. Though this book *could* help everyone, not everyone is ready for help. Just think about alcoholics: they need to hit a bottom before they are ready to make a change in their lives. Some of them never hit it. Some of them are forced to change by friends and family, but it doesn't take long for them to drink again because they didn't want it for themselves.

Also know the path of least resistance probably contradicts a lifestyle you currently lead, which means it will take you out of your comfort zone. It is outside of your comfort zone where you will find the greatest growth and achievement. I'll discuss this more soon, but first I would like you to write something down. Don't worry; you can go grab a piece of paper and a pen. I'll be here when you get back.

See, I'm still here. What I want you to write down is why you need to live an Oscar-worthy life. Why do you need to be the best person you can be? Why do you need to be an outstanding actor?

You may have noticed the wording of my questions is not the norm. Most people ask why you *want* something but wants can be justified if you don't obtain them. I have wanted things in the past, a new car, a new job, a girlfriend. When I didn't get what I wanted, I provided reasons why I shouldn't or didn't obtain it: *a new car would be too expensive anyway, the job I have is close to home and it isn't that bad, I probably wouldn't be able to hang out with my other friends if I had a girlfriend.* I'm sure you have said these things or something similar at one time or another. We don't make the same excuses for things we need. We beg, borrow, steal, cheat, and lie for those things.

So, when you write down why you need to live an Oscar-worthy life or why you need to be an outstanding actor, know it has to be a strong enough reason to contemplate doing any of those immoral and illegal things. You won't have to. As a matter of fact, it would only work against you to do so, but know it has to be a need.

ACTOR'S NOTE: WHEN ANALYZING YOUR SCRIPTS, USE THE PHRASE "I NEED" AS OPPOSED TO "I WANT".

We do what we do in life to fulfill our needs. So this is the perfect place to start. If we know why we do the things we do, we can recreate the process without any problems. You become an actor by taking action.

NEED THE DOUGH

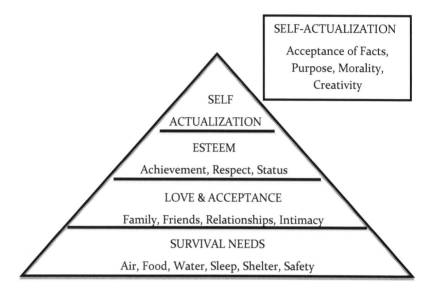

There are basic human needs. Abraham Maslow (a psychologist) formulated them into a pyramid. I've restructured the pyramid slightly in order to simplify it.

The foundation of the original pyramid is *physiological* or *physical needs*, which means having to do with our body, but as you notice, I've renamed the foundational tier *survival needs* combining the two foundational tiers because everything in the original pyramid's first two tiers: air, food, water, sleep, clothing, shelter, safety have to do with our basic survival. Our first need is self-preservation. It is a basic human instinct. It is innate. We are born with this programmed into every cell of our body. The closer a need is to our foundation, the greater the weight it has in our minds and we will fight for it more.

So, when I wanted a new car, it didn't fulfill one of the foundational needs. I had a vehicle or could've used the bus to get where I needed to go, but travel isn't a need. When I needed to get somewhere, I was willing to walk. I would have had to equate the vehicle to a need for survival; it would have to be a need to obtain my other needs for survival.

The next tier is the need for love and acceptance. Remember this:

Love and acceptance lead to transcendence. (Here is a quotable statement – I told you it would be quotable)

I know what you're thinking. This guy is trying to sound profound. I'm not; it is just pure dumb luck when it happens. I actually wrote this book to break down the profundity of life, so you have an easy path for success. That is not to say you won't have to do work, but if you train hard, you succeed easy. You put in the work before the game, before the competition, before life happens and all obstacles will disappear because your mind will not view them as obstacles. If you live hard, laugh hard, love hard, then when the opportunity arises for you to shine, you will.

I once wrote a poem about a prostitute when I was twenty; it was for an English class I was taking. I like to write about taboo topics and shock my audience.

I had not experienced one at the time (and still haven't) but this thought crossed my mind. *Why would I pay to have sex with someone when I could just masturbate for free?* It was a legitimate question and it sparked an internal debate that lasted a week while I wrote the poem (which can be found at the end of the book). I realized people don't pay for sex. They pay for attention. I later confirmed this when I spoke with strippers and former prostitutes who said a lot of customers didn't want sex at all. They just wanted someone to talk to. They wanted to feel loved and accepted for who they were. The ones who wanted sex just equated sex to love. After all, affection is the greatest sign of love and sex is the greatest form affection.

The lesson I'm trying to teach you before the lessons is everything we do (outside of just trying to survive), we do for those two reasons and those two reasons alone. It all boils down to love and acceptance. The job you have, the car you drive, the spouse you've chosen all have a common denominator: They have provided you with or you thought they would provide you with love and acceptance from a person or group of people that you hold in high esteem.

We are constantly trying to win the favor of someone or fit in with a group of people, so much so we change our style, our personality, and sometimes go as far as changing our beliefs.

Gangs are a great example. Most gang members are raised by single mothers. Subconsciously, they seek out the love and acceptance from father figures. Higher tier gang members recruit new members with the same tactics that were used on them, the promise of a family that will love and accept them. Children, in this case, boys whose fathers are absent, believe their fathers left because they didn't love them, so when offered the opportunity to be loved and accepted by a male figure, they often jump at the opportunity no matter what the cost. I'm sure they believe killing is wrong, but people have committed and will continue to commit murder to fulfill their needs.

This is an extreme example of fulfilling a need, but realize when something is a need as opposed to a want, we will go to the extreme to obtain it, not to say the extreme is right.

ACTOR'S NOTE: IN ACTING, THERE ARE NO RIGHT OR WRONG CHOICES, JUST WEAK AND STRONG CHOICES. THE STRONGEST CHOICE IS ALWAYS THE ONE WHICH IS THE DIFFERENCE BETWEEN LIFE AND DEATH. THE FARTHER DOWN ON THE PYRAMID OF NEEDS YOUR CHOICE IS, THE STRONGER THE CHOICE. MORE ON THIS LATER.

IT HURTS SO GOOD

In order to obtain what you haven't had, you need to do things that you haven't done. This is going to be uncomfortable. Accept this, for confusion and comfort kill. If we are not growing, we are decaying, and if we are to grow we must always be in a constant state of discomfort. Reading this book is providing growth, discomfort, and clarity. All of these are causing you to live, live in this moment, now. The moment you become passive in your life and let life act upon you, you are the semblance of death. There is a beautiful but pertinent cliché which states, NO PAIN, NO GAIN. This is a direct reference to physical fitness, building muscle. Here is the thing: the heart is a muscle; the brain is a muscle (not medically speaking for all the nerds who are going to try and correct me). Without any pain in our life, we wouldn't grow. We would just decay and we know that is death.

Where am I going with this? Great question. I'm not here to judge you but rather I want you to evaluate your daily rituals. Do they lend themselves one hundred percent to your success? My guess is they don't because I've been there. On occasion I still go there. I'm not perfect; no one is asking you to be. I'm just going to give you some insight on how to dedicate yourself to your imperfections and succeed in spite of them. There are some things we need to work on though, because it is about what you know before it's about whom you know.

I want you to become very familiar with these words: *weirdo, crazy, nut job, oddball, stupid, sucker, flake, cracked, mad, silly, mental, idiot, dummy, fool,* and any other word that insinuates you are not normal. You will be called plenty of these words. If you have been called any one of these because of your ideas and your dreams, you are already on the right path.

Walt Disney, the gentleman who shaped many childhoods and gave us the permission to dream, was a weirdo. When Walt tried to get MGM studios to distribute Mickey Mouse in 1927 he was told that the idea would never work—a giant mouse on the screen would terrify women. Mickey is now iconic.

Here is a list of others who not only went outside their comfort zones but also were chastised and criticized for thinking outside of the box. Everyone probably knows most of these 'once' failures and revolutionary thinkers. You only know them because they not only thought outside their comfort zone but also acted outside of it.

-Winston Churchill

-J.K. Rowling

-Fred Astaire

-Oprah Winfrey

-Harrison Ford

-Thomas Edison

-Stephen Spielberg

-Soichiro Honda

-Henry Ford

-Albert Einstein

-Steve Jobs

Your mind is the reason a comfort zone exists in the first place. Your mind likes to protect you from pain. As a matter of fact, subconsciously, we choose avoidance of pain over gaining pleasure.

Let us take our NO PAIN, NO GAIN example again. In order for us to achieve the health we 'want' we would 'need' to work out. Working out causes pain. The harder you work, the more pain you feel.

I remember the first time I went to college (I went more than once). The guys that I cliqued with were jocks. I was a jock in high school, but not to their extreme. Wanting to be accepted by them, I agreed to go work out with them when they invited me. They were not only lifting some major weight, but also doing major reps. I wanted to fit in (love and acceptance, right?), so I pushed as hard as I possibly could without having a hernia or dislocating limbs. When I woke up the next morning, I couldn't move my arms, literally. It hurt so badly. I went to breakfast and cried, sitting at the table, looking as if I was holding an invisible five-foot boulder. My muscles were a little bigger and a lot tighter. It took me three days to get limber again. I didn't work out much after that. My mind always reminded me of the pain that I endured.

Now, I would definitely gain pleasure from being healthy, and when I say healthy, I don't mean just a great cholesterol level. I mean a six-pack and some guns. I would draw more attention. I would gain more affection. I would be able to be more active and enjoy life without any discomfort, but the thought of pain kept me from exercising.

The thought of pain kept me from doing a lot of things in my life. We only change when the pain is too much to handle, the pain of being broke, or the pain of being homeless, or the pain of loneliness. We act when we want to avoid a greater pain than what we are avoiding. We basically choose the lesser of the two evils.

People don't like to diet and watch what they eat. Eating provides comfort. Which means that not eating would be outside your comfort zone. So, people eat and eat unhealthily, until they receive the news from their doctors that they have high blood pressure, high cholesterol, or diabetes. They are informed that these can lead to strokes, amputation, blindness, and even death. Those pains are greater than the pain of exercising and dieting, so what do they do? They change their eating habits; they work out. Realize they are not making that choice because they are gaining pleasure in being healthy. They make the choice because they want to avoid greater pain.

So, what is going to make you do something you do not want to do? Knowing the pain you will experience if you do not do it will be worse than what you are currently experiencing.

ACTOR'S NOTE: AS AN ACTOR, THE BEST WAY TO GROW AND GET OUT OF YOUR COMFORT ZONE IS TO BE VULNERABLE. WE DON'T LIKE TO FEEL ANGRY, SAD, OR FRIGHTENED BECAUSE THOSE EMOTIONS SHOW WE ARE WEAK. GUESS WHAT? WE ARE WEAK BECAUSE WE ARE HUMAN. NO ONE EVER WANTS TO SHOW THEY ARE WEAK, BUT WHEN YOU DO, PEOPLE RESPECT THE STRENGTH IT TOOK TO DO IT.

I Urge You To Suck

There are very few things we are able to do when we come out of the womb: cry, poop, and suck. Eventually, we are taught not to suck, not to be a sucker; suckers are bad. I don't like to sit on the same side of the fence as the majority. I think sucking is good; especially as Thoreau explained it:

I went to the woods because I wished to live deliberately, to front only the essential facts of life, and see if I could not learn what it had to teach, and not, when I came to die, discover that I had not lived. I did not wish to live what was not life, living is so dear; nor did I wish to practice resignation, unless it was quite necessary. I wanted to live deep and suck out all the marrow of life, to live so sturdily and Spartan-like as to put to rout all that was not life, to cut a broad swath and shave close, to drive life into a corner, and reduce it to its lowest terms.

As a baby your mother took advantage of your sucking. It eased the pain in her breasts. You took advantage of her because it provided you with sustenance. Whether or not you believe it, we are here to ease the suffering of others. When people suck from you, realize you are providing life. It's really a misnomer to call the person who loses at three-card Monte a sucker. The sucker is the one sucking life from the player. Most people would call you *stupid, gullible, or a sucker*. I would call you *unfocused*. Do not

19

worry. We all lose focus. It is a habit which we have to build, focusing. When we remain focused we live with more purpose. We may live like Thoreau.

I wish to do the exact same thing, which is why I have broken down living an Oscar-worthy life into the lowest terms so all who may wish to succeed may do so. Do not learn not to suck; learn to suck deliberately. When you live with purpose and act to help others, you will never feel like a sucker. You will feel fulfilled. You may even feel like you are taking advantage of people because they are bringing you life.

ACTOR'S NOTE: THE MORE DELIBERATELY YOU LIVE THE MORE EXPERIENCES YOU'LL HAVE TO PULL FROM FOR YOUR CHARACTERS.

YOU KNOW WHAT...

It's not what you know but whom you know. Is it really? Let's say I'm a very important person, which I am, and you know me. If you don't me, my name is Dorian Alexis Santiago, and my number is 470.222.6447. Feel free to contact me at your leisure, but I'm going to ask you some pertinent questions when you call.

- With whom am I speaking?
- How are you?
- How can I help you?
- What do you know how to do?

I'm hoping the first answer is easy for you: a name will suffice, no title needed, unless you have a really ambiguous voice and name, then a Mr. or Ms. would be extremely helpful to avoid any awkward moments on your side.

I'm hoping the second answer is not only easy but also positive. As much as I care about you, I know the extent of my abilities to help *everyone* (which is minimal). I know negative people are not successful unless they inherited some wealth, and I assure you, they don't maintain their success with a negative mindset. They either change or they lose it.

Your third answer is a setup. Remember, I know how to be a sucker. I am looking to find out if you know how to be a sucker. After you have told me your "brief" story, I'll ask, "What do you know how to do?" "What have you done to help yourself?" Realize I won't ask whom you know because I'm already speaking with the most important person in the conversation.

Now, I understand that we all need a little help. No one who is successful has done it alone. I promise you. Even as you read this, I am helping you with my knowledge and insight of my experience. So you are not going about your journey alone. I did not reach this level by myself, but my efforts surpassed the next person and were noticed by others who are successful. I also do not sling words like *dedication, loyalty, determination, punctuality,* and *integrity* around like a chimp slings his poop. If you do, know this does not serve you well. Successful people hold these virtues and principles in high esteem and will call you on it.

Your last answer really is the most important. If you don't have a skill set, the minimum you must know is the virtues and principles to learn one.

I am aware that it is exactly what I know that leads me to who I know. If I know business, I meet business people, business owners, and executives. If I know literature, I meet writers, authors, and wordsmiths. If I am an actor, I meet actors, directors, and producers. The level of knowledge you have is a direct correlation to the level of person you'll meet in your field.

If you know little. You meet little people (this is not a midget joke). You know a lot. You meet the elite.

ACTOR'S NOTE: I'VE FOUND THAT THE MAJORITY OF ACTORS FEEL LIKE THAT HAVE TO DO SOMETHING DIFFERENT WHEN GOING TO CLASS. THE WORLD IS OUR GYM, OUR PLAYGROUND. WE ARE ACTORS. AS AN ACTING COACH, I CANNOT TEACH YOU HOW TO BE HUMAN. YOU JUST ARE. WHAT I CAN TEACH YOU IS NOT ONLY HOW TO BE A BETTER HUMAN, BUT MAKE YOU AWARE OF WHAT YOU ALREADY DO AS A HUMAN THAT MOVES PEOPLE.

FOCUS

You may often try to convince yourself that you deserve something, but if that were the case, then you'd have it. The people who are truly devoted receive what they want. You know their names: Mark Zuckerberg, Bill Gates, Barack Obama. They chose their goal and have lived to achieve it. If you believe you achieve.

You might be saying at this moment you have dedicated yourself to your goal. *Ha!* I'm not laughing at you. I'm laughing at your perception of dedication. All the stories of successful people I have heard and read have taught me you don't stop learning and doing and learning until you have achieved what you want; then they realized that it worked and they learned and did more. Their dedication led to immense struggle because they were willing to sacrifice everything, including comfort to succeed. Is your comfort more important than your goal? Are you not sure?

I decided when I started my journey to come to terms with the fact I may wind up being homeless and living out of my vehicle.

REMEMBER:
ALL THE WORLD IS A STAGE AND WE ARE MERELY JUST PLAYERS
(ACTORS).

PRODUCTION

Most coaches (life or acting) try to teach you techniques that you already do. There is no need to teach you any technique. There is no technique on how to recreate humanity; rather, if you are aware when you are moved most in life, you can focus on those moments to generate the strongest emotion for your character, take the greatest action steps, and touch the most lives.

IMPROVIZENTION

Welcome obedient readers. If you just skipped the introduction, we can't have that. I didn't put important information in it for you to just ignore it. So, go back right now and read it. I reference the information often.

Basketball. Even after rupturing both of my Achilles' tendons, playing basketball puts me in a state of Zen. I become lost in the game, in the moment. I don't think about anything else going on in my life. Playing basketball quiets my mind. I am aware of everything taking place on the court. I am present.

This is ZEN.

The majority of people can relate some hobby, sport, or extracurricular activity in their life to this feeling. It is defined as 'Mindfulness'. Before I go any further, I want you to know ZEN is not a religion, just in case you thought I was going to try and convert you. I'm not. ZEN is a philosophy, which is defined as the most basic beliefs, concepts, and attitudes of an individual or group. It is much like capitalism, racism, and feminism. The concept behind ZEN is that if you are present in the moment, you become enlightened. You gain knowledge. Simple.

With knowledge there is clarity; with clarity we are able to act deliberately. Without clarity, we have confusion. Confusion kills, it causes hesitation. We have all nearly killed or have killed an animal in the road. We notice the squirrel. The squirrel has a goal: to get to the other side of the road. The squirrel hears something, feels something but isn't clear on what it is. It's confused and in its confusion, it hesitates. It thinks. *Do I continue crossing or go back?* That moment, that single solitary moment of confusion is the reason it is road kill. It could have made the decision to go back, failing to reach its goal. It would have had to live with the failure or it would decide to reach its goal.

We are squirrels, except our distractions are not vehicles, but voices. They sound like our family, our friends, our spouses. They focus on the past, on pain, on fear, on the future. They create confusion and cause us to hesitate, and we do, for years. The only way we can move is by staying in the moment. Being present. Taking one step at a time and focusing on the step you are taking. If you look behind you or in front, you will doubt yourself. You will convince yourself you haven't gone as far as you thought. You will convince yourself your goal is too far away. If you focus on the step you are taking, if you are present, if you are living in that moment, then success will appear.

A woman whom I loved dearly was scared of the future. We were happy together when we stayed present with each other. I told her if you just focus on this moment, the moments will accumulate and fifty years from now you will have known nothing but happiness. You will also know nothing but happiness if you focus on this moment, live in this moment, are happy in this moment. Be present. This is ImproviZENtion.

Life is ImproviZENtion. We receive phone calls, meet new people, and experience unexpected encounters that we have to deal with in the moment. Jokes, hugs, and awkward moments aren't thought out. They just happen because we don't know what is going to happen from one moment to the next. We don't know how someone is going to react to what we are going to say. We don't know how any conversation is going to flow at any given time. ImproviZENtion is acting, which leads me back to my initial statement: LIFE IS ACTING, ACTING IS LIFE. The rules are simple and if followed you'll attain success in your life and career, especially if your career is acting. If you follow the principles, you'll attain it much quicker than most. Remember, if you master the rules and principles of one, you've mastered the rules and principles of both. Also remember though, knowledge is worthless without application. Apply what I'm telling you and your life will shine.

RULES

RULE #1
DO NOT DENY!

No! Just looking at the word for less than a second releases dozens of stress-producing hormones. *No!* These disrupt normal brain function, logic, reason, language processing, and communication. *No!* If you think that is bad, it is even worse when we hear it. It makes us irritable and anxious. We tend not to cooperate with those who tell us *No.* We also lose trust in the person who has said it, whether it is family, friends or co-workers. *No! No! No!* I've said it enough for the rest of my life and yours, so let's not say it anymore.

The rule just isn't about not saying the word. It is about acceptance. ***Acceptance is key***. Accept all that life has to offer; accept that life may be unfair; accept that the only constant in life is change and the only thing you can change is yourself; accept you play a part in your current situation and only you have the power to change it. If we don't hold ourselves accountable for our decisions, our actions, and our lives then we can't change them. It all starts with acceptance.

Acceptance is acknowledgement not abdication. It doesn't mean you have to surrender but rather embrace. Theoretically for this analogy, I will say death is the enemy of life and what do we do with our enemies? We fight. What happens when we fight our enemies, injury and death; we either kill them or they kill us. Now, if we embrace them then war is prevented, no one has to die or surrender. For all of you thinking about the extremists, remember they are doing what they are doing for the same reasons I stated before, love and acceptance. If you don't acknowledge death is imminent then you fail to live; you believe you have all the time in the world to do whatever it is you may want to do. Non-acceptance makes you a prisoner.

We all love; we all lose; we all die. Accept this. We are all human, so rich people are no different than poor people. They have the same problems; they just think they can fix them with money.

There are certain things in life that we cannot change, they are predetermined and established. These are what are referred to as universal laws; they contain what we more commonly know as the laws of physics, mathematics, and biology. To try and change them is a waste of energy. By simply understanding and accepting them, we can work with them to progress.

This works with other established information, for example, you have a boss. I've had bosses who were not as intelligent as me. They weren't as creative. They weren't as driven. I was so focused on how someone like him could be in his position, and I fought against his position in power that I wasn't as productive as I could have been. The company didn't do any better with me there. If I had changed my focus, worked with him, made some amazing developments in the company, I would have excelled in my position and the company.

Accept that you are not perfect. If we were born perfect, then there wouldn't be any need to live. After all, living is growing. If you are fully grown and perfect, there is no place to go. I've always enjoyed the fact that I am perfectly imperfect or imperfectly perfect. I am a perfect human. I am the best me at any given moment and as I grow, my best me becomes better. Be the best you and the only way to do that is accept yourself for being human. Don't consider yourself flawed but rather underdeveloped and accept the fact others are the same.

ACTOR'S RECAP: ACCEPTANCE OF ESTABLISHED INFORMATION IS KEY TO OUTSTANDING IMPROV. IT PROGRESSES A SCENE BECAUSE WE AREN'T FIGHTING OUR PARTNER BUT RATHER WORKING WITH THEM. NO ONE CARES TO WATCH BICKERING. CONFLICT IS DIFFERENT THAN BICKERING. ACCEPT AND PROGRESS OR DENY AND DIE. DON'T KILL YOUR SCENE.

RULE #2
BE LEGITIMATE

This has nothing to do with having parents who were married when you were conceived and/or born. It is okay if they weren't. This has everything to do where you live. As for myself, I live in the greatest city in the universe, AUTHENTICITY. That's right. I'm a cornball on occasion. I embrace it and because I do, so do others. You are most powerful when you are true to yourself. This happens when you release the doubt and fear that you, the real you is worthy of love and acceptance. This happens when you don't let the criticism of others affect your life. This happens when you accept the fact that you are imperfectly perfect and human. This happens when you allow yourself to be vulnerable.

It is understandable that we don't like to be vulnerable; we don't want to appear weak. We are born with a natural instinct to protect ourselves from harm and death. It is the instinct of self-preservation. It is the reason that people lie, steal, cheat, and kill. We are animals, and we are wired as such. Our primal nature tells us to take first and kill anything that threatens us. We actually are taught to become civil. The way we have become civil is by creating defense mechanisms that don't lead to violence.

Defense mechanisms are the masks we wear to hide our real emotions, the ones that reveal our vulnerability. Our masks almost become our true selves, but I know I am self-deprecating because I don't want to show that something someone has said might have hurt. It doesn't normally because I value myself, but if something does hurt, I'm happy to state that out loud. I am okay with informing the sender of such information it hurt, showing I'm vulnerable. As I've matured, I've learned to combat these moments with understanding, coming to terms they are either trying to connect with me and don't want to admit that because it shows vulnerability on their part or they are not happy with themselves which would also show vulnerability, so they mask it with insults.

Most of the world equates vulnerability to weakness. Weakness is the opposite of strength, but it takes a very strong person to purposefully reveal their weakness. After all, weakness and vulnerability are parts of being human. We connect with others on the deepest levels when we are vulnerable. Think of when we are most vulnerable: when someone close to us dies. That is when most people will reach out because again, we're connected in life through death, and that makes us all vulnerable and human.

The only people who like douche bags are other douche bags, and sometimes even they don't like themselves.

ACTOR RECAP: BE AUTHENTIC. THE WORST THING YOU CAN DO IS PRETEND. PRETENDING IS TIRESOME. YOU'LL QUICKLY COME OUT OF YOUR CHARACTER IF YOU ARE PRETENDING. IT TAKES MORE WORK TO WEAR A MASK THAN TO JUST BE AUTHENTIC.

RULE #3
SHOW US, DON'T TELL US

I'm from Missouri; you're going to have to show me. Do not speak unless it improves upon silence. Actions speak louder than words, right? We have all heard numerous quotes on this topic. Nike would be a far less successful company if their marketing slogan was *Just Say It.* Eighty percent of information we take in is through our vision, so it's time to show up, show out, and show us.

This is probably the simplest rule in life, but my actors make it difficult. In life, we tend to talk a good game but rarely take action.

In order for people to take notice, we have to act. Words are empty. We remark on events and situations where we would've liked to have done something. We don't stand up for ourselves because of fear. We talk a lot. This book is not a result of talking. It is a result of sitting down and researching, writing, and having it published. We are not our words but our actions.

We fail to act because of fear. It is much easier to state something and never take action, but those who act are highly respected and successful individuals. Do we not respect Donald Trump, Oprah Winfrey, Bill Gates, Angela Merkel (look her up), and Michael Jordan? Why? They showed us.

Poor, unsuccessful people have the following mentality: I'll believe it when I see it. They need to see proof. If you show them, they believe; they follow. Successful people have an opposing mentality: I see it because I believe it. They are leaders, innovators. You have to act in order for people to see. After all, actions do speak louder than words. This is not to say words aren't effective.

Words move the mind/heart, but actions move the body/soul. We have all heard that words are powerful. The truth is words are only as powerful as the action taken with them. Dr.

Martin Luther King's words would've have been useless if he didn't live what he spoke.

I've never been afraid of someone who likes to verbally threaten. They are scared. They are trying to avoid physical confrontation through empty threats. A gentleman who told me he was a high priest in voodoo once threatened me. I called *bullshit*. People who intend to hurt you, hurt you. There isn't any talking. It just happens. A great example of this is the mafia; no threats, just death.

We are more fearful of people who act rather than talk, which means that if you take action, people will realize you are serious and work with you rather than against you. There is a respect for someone who acts.

I love *Braveheart*. William Wallace was a legend who was highly respected and also feared. What's the difference? Respect is looked at as positive while fear is viewed as negative. William Wallace was respected by his followers. He reinforced all his words with action. This is what created fear in his enemies. It is one thing to promise, but if you don't deliver on your promise you lose all credibility.

Let's use a visual. For this visual < stands for fear and > stands for respect.

English soldiers < William Wallace > his army.

Most people will argue that fear and respect can coexist. Of course they can but not in the same person at the same time for the same subject. This isn't possible. If you respect someone because of the harm they can cause you, then you fear them. You just use the term respect so you don't come across as weak. English soldiers didn't respect William Wallace, they feared him. They planned all their strategies not because they respected his power, but feared it. If the English respected William Wallace, his dedication to the freedom of his people, they would've taken a different stance and in admiration they would've conceded to this virtue.

Fear and respect have everything to do with the recipient's view of someone's actions not their words.

I remember joining my mother and a group of her friends at a restaurant one evening. She had been in recovery for almost a year, but I still resented her for putting me through hell while she was drinking. There were around 20 people and everyone was listening to her. She was magnet and I hated it. I wanted everyone to dislike her the way I did. Did they not know how she used to be?

The gentleman she was seeing at the time saw I purposefully removed myself from the group, so he came to talk with me. In our brief discussion, I asked what he saw in my mother; what was it they everyone liked about her. The answer was simple.

She was real.

She said what she meant; she meant what she said and she wasn't afraid to show you who she really was. She didn't give a shit if you liked her or didn't because she came to the realization that if she didn't show you who she was, the real her, she would drink again. She showed her feelings. She didn't just talk about them. That brief conversation shed a new light on my mother and I gained a new found respect for her.

Take action. Commit and move forward deliberately. The only way you will be able to do this is by accepting and being true to yourself. Thanks Mom.

ACTOR'S RECAP: DON'T TELL THE AUDIENCE HOW YOU ARE FEELING OR WHAT YOU ARE DOING. SHOW THEM. REMEMBER, SOME OF THE GREATEST ACTING WAS DONE IN SILENT FILMS.

RULE #4
STAY IN THE MOMENT

Actively listen. The word *listen* is built with the same letters as 'silent'.

We live in a world of commodities, natural resources, and materials. The only one that is limited and irreplaceable is time, but yet we waste it on a daily basis letting problems consume it; the only way not to let that happen is to be more conscious of each moment.

As stated before, life is made up of moments, and each moment lived to its full potential creates momentum. That's right. *Momentum*. The root of the word comes from the word *moment*. If we continue to put energy into each moment, we build momentum.

Success likes speed; as a matter of fact, everything likes speed. Speed makes things go smoother. You'll go further, faster. Momentum will create residual energy. They say slow and steady wins the race. I call bullshit. Even the greatest marathon runners average a four and three quarter minute mile, which is for twenty-six point two miles. The only thing that doesn't like speed is women when it comes to the length of time from foreplay to orgasm for men. As a wildebeest if you want to survive, you just have to be faster than the slowest. Eventually though, you'll be the slowest. If don't just want to survive, but succeed and lead, you have to be the fastest.

In order to build momentum, we have to live fully in each moment, for there is nothing as important as this moment. Only in this moment do we grow, do we succeed. This moment is fleeting, so use it wisely. Realize that you are reading history. This book was written in the moments of which I took advantage. This book didn't happen in the past of the future. It happened in the present. Your reading this book isn't happening in the past or the future. It is happening in the now. Action takes place in the present. I cannot act in the past. I cannot undo an action nor can I change an action that has not yet occurred. My power lies in this moment. I am defined by this moment, which is why you are able to read this.

A body in motion will remain in motion unless acted upon by an outside force. That outside force comes in the form of haters, the naysayers, and the people who don't want you to succeed. These people, along with others from your past who may have had good intentions, restrict you. They appear as a little voice in your head. Remember when we have the choice, we will avoid pain rather than gain pleasure. The little voice inside your head will continue to give you reasons not to do it.

So, the greatest problem here is the how. I can tell you what you need to do, but what stops everyone from action is the "I don't know how". ACTING IS LIFE, AND LIFE IS ACTING. Who has given you the instruction manual on how to live? If you have one, how well has it worked out for you? If there were one, would you take it? If you did, your life would be mundane and boring. It is the challenges of not knowing that keep us growing. Getting back to the matter at hand, no one has given you an instruction book, but some people have provided some guidance and advice specifically based upon their experiences. We just live. We go through our day and face each challenge as it comes.

I remember having a discussion with my ex-wife. I really wanted to have children, and she had already had a child, who was exceptional, but he was already in his tweens when we met. Anyway, we had this discussion about if we had children, when would I feel comfortable leaving my child. I'm a rational man. I loved my ex-wife. I figured after my child's first steps, I would be okay taking a week-

long vacation to insure that I also gave my wife the attention I believe she deserved. I realize that we wear many hats and if you commit to one, you lose your identity as a person. I wasn't just going to be a father. I was still going to be a husband, and an individual. She didn't care for the answer and subsequently, we never had children.

The point is this. I don't care how much I discussed something. When the time came to be a father and live in that moment. I might have made a different decision; I could only speak from a hypothetical point of view. I still believe that I could have the same argument today, but nothing prepares us for the actual event or day. We can prepare all we want, but when the day starts, we have to face what it brings us the best way we know how.

So you want to know how you stay in the moment, here are the directions:

1. Listen.
2. Listen.
3. Listen some more.
4. Respond.

There it is. I know that may seem extremely simple and it is, but applying it is the difficult part because we get in our own way. We over analyze; we let the voices in our mind take over; we dismiss moments instead of embracing them and the opportunity they are providing for growth.

Listen to this; listen to me; listen to others; listen to the universe; most of all, listen to yourself, your intuition, your higher conscience. The universe is constantly speaking to you, guiding you towards your purpose. Pay attention to the lessons it wants to teach you.

ACTOR'S RECAP: ACTIVELY LISTEN. THE MOST IMPORTANT INFORMATION IN THE SCENE IS WHAT COMES IN, NOT WHAT GOES OUT. THE WAY WE STAY IN THE MOMENT IS TO MAKE THE SCENE ABOUT YOUR PARTNER.

Along with the four main rules of Improv, there are also numerous principles. The difference between a rule and principle is this; rules are enforced by an outside source. They are in place for a system to work properly. Principles come from within and by applying them, systems don't just work properly, they become efficient and flourish, e.g. Rule – *Hold someone's hand when you're crossing the street*, Principle – *Be safe.* Principles are values. Here are the principles of Improv that will make your life, personal and professional, outstanding. These are in order of what I believe is most important. Realize they aren't complex, but they can be difficult when we resist them. Focus on execution not excuses.

Principles

PRINCIPLE #1
CARE

You have to care about other people more than yourself. Do you realize that if you help other people fulfill their dreams, your dreams will also be fulfilled? I am an acting coach. The actors I've coached have won many awards. One day, I know I will be able to say that I coached an Academy Award Winner. What if one day I'm able to say I coach every Academy Award winner? Helping them fulfill their dreams and become successful makes me successful. Everyone will want to be coached by me. I won't be able to keep up with the workload, because everyone will know that if you want to win an Academy Award, you should be coached by Dorian Santiago.

You have to genuinely care. May I quickly reference Rule #2 (BE LEGITIMATE). People will eventually know that you are a fake or phony. If you don't care about people, don't fake it, but there has to be a group of people that you do care for and not just because they can help you. Care about them because you can help them. We are here to help and serve others. You do it on a daily basis but we aren't conscious of it. We just do our jobs to do our jobs, but let's quickly look at a job and see how it helps and serves others.

I worked in customer service for a long time before I decided to change my life's path. I am great at it. The reason: I care. I want to solve problems for people. It gives me purpose. The problems I was solving just happened to be the ones that my company (the one I worked for) created.

The first of the Four Noble Truths of Zen philosophy states *Life is suffering*. We are here to prevent and reduce suffering of others. The only way to do this is by caring. Now back to my customer service job, my company sold children's rainwear. We want our children to stay dry. Being wet can cause suffering. Parents reduce the suffering of their children. Something happens to the raincoat and the child cannot wear it. The child suffers. The parent suffers because the child suffers. It was my job to ease the suffering of both. We all have problems. They are only as big as the amount of energy we give to them.

*ACTOR'S RECAP: **THE STRONGEST CHOICE YOU CAN MAKE AS AN ACTOR IS TO CARE. FIND A REASON. THE PERSON IN THE SCENE WITH YOU FULFILLS A NEED, SO CARE. IF YOU DON'T CARE, THEY DON'T CARE, AND THE AUDIENCE CERTAINLY WON'T CARE.***

PRINCIPLE #2
ESTABLISH A RELATIONSHIP

We do things for people we like and we do even more for the people we love. In a perfect world, we would all love each other and like each other, but that isn't the case. So, we have to start somewhere and build.

Follow the yellow the brick road. For those of you not familiar with this line, you might want to do more than just read this book because again whom you know depends greatly on what you know. *The Wizard of Oz* is a classic movie. I could get into all the life lessons it teaches, but I'll save that for another book. For this principle, I strictly want to focus on the yellow brick road. It is the foundation for all of Dorothy's relationships. She is going to see the wizard, the wonderful Wizard of Oz because of the wonderful things he does (see what I did there?).

Her relationships were fortified immediately because she established a connection with the other characters. They all were suffering. She suffered from homesickness, she wanted her family; the Tin Man suffered from a lack of emotion, he wanted love. The Scarecrow suffered from a lack of intelligence, he wanted knowledge; and the Lion suffered from fear; he wanted courage.

Dorothy connected with them on this level and offered them a way to ease their suffering. That genuine connection built trust and relationships that lasted a lifetime or at least until the end of the book. By helping them reach their goals, she was able to achieve hers. The obstacles she encountered would not have been overcome without the help of the relationships she nurtured.

We are all human first. So, I've made this super easy for you. You already have an established relationship to everyone in the world. We are connected through the First Noble Truth, suffering. The problem is we quickly are taught exclusion and sub-cultures and we lose sight of being connected to everyone in the world on a grander scale. We label each other and ourselves and move along this path called life in a box. We look for instant fixes and fail to give anyone our time that doesn't seem to provide immediate gratification.

What has a stranger ever done for you to bring you closer to your goals? There may be a small number of people who have received a blessing from a stranger that was life changing to the point of success, but they probably aren't reading this book. If you are, I'd love to hear your story. You see, because we've lost our sense of humanity; we don't help others who can't help us. We have this survival of the fittest mentality and with it comes extreme selfishness. Who has helped you most in your life? That's right. You can say it, people with whom you have a strong relationship. Their love for you fuels their actions. I am a philanthropic person, but I can only help so many people because my resources and more importantly my time are limited. So, the stronger my relationship is to you, the more likely I'm going to help you.

ACTORS RECAP: THERE ARE NO RIGHT OR WRONG CHOICES, JUST WEAK AND STRONG ONES. THE STRONGEST CHOICES COME FROM STRONG RELATIONSHIPS. ESTABLISH RELATIONSHIPS QUICKLY IN YOUR IMPROV AND MAKE THEM STRONGEST ONES; AND NOT JUST TO PEOPLE BUT OBJECTS. CHOOSING TO BE BEST FRIENDS IS A MUCH STRONGER CHOICE THAN JUST FRIENDS. A WATCH YOU'RE WEARING BELONGING TO YOUR GREAT, GREAT GRANDFATHER IS A SUPER STRONG CHOICE COMPARED TO A WATCH YOU JUST FOUND.

PRINCIPLE #3
BE ENERGETIC

Everything is energy: thoughts, words, and actions. Everything. The more energy you put into a relationship, project, or product, the greater the return.

A lack of energy shows a lack of interest, and a lack of interest means you don't care (Reference Principle #1 CARE). All of these principles are connected, just like all of us. I love science. It is fascinating. There is a theory of something or other that states energy in equals energy out. The statement is only partially true. In order for it to be completely true, you have to have a closed system in thermal equilibrium. I know...I thought the same thing as I read it...*blah, blah, blah*, so moving on.

Energy is defined as the capacity for work or power. I want to make this very clear, without work you have no power. Success is not easy. It takes work. The work you do may seem to go unnoticed, but it isn't. The universe notices. I'm sure you've heard about 'The Secret' because it isn't much of a secret any more, and in my opinion it never really was a secret. The problem is most people don't want to hear it. They don't feel worthy of hearing the secret. I'm sure many people have said, "Why would you tell me?" or "That won't work for me." These words are not the secret to success but rather the secret to distress.

So, let me clarify this principle: I don't want you to just put energy into your dreams and goals; you have to put positive energy into them. Negative energy kills.

This book is energy. As you hold it, know that the energy within it is being transferred to you. If that energy isn't enough, burn it. It may keep you warm for five minutes. Energy. The return I have received and the product of my energy is going to be visible in lives of the people that read this book.

Basketball, again. I like basketball because it requires a lot of energy, so much that there are frequent substitutions in order to keep the team at its peak potential. Teams train often in order to produce efficient energy burning players. The longer a player can maintain a high level of energy the better, especially if he is an all-star, and most of them are.

All-stars don't drag ass, they rarely complain, and they always put the most energy into being the best they can be. Be aware that you will have to maintain a high level of energy to keep up with the world, because people are going to feed off of your energy.

You can instantly tell how great a play, concert, or any other live performance or activity is going to be because of the energy that you feel in the air. It is the energy from the performers, athletes, etc...

This principle, along with many of the others, falls into the law of reciprocity; what you sow, so shall you reap. If you care, others care. If you are energetic, others will be energetic. This is fairly simple: the problem is we don't apply it.

ACTOR'S RECAP: ENERGY EQUATES TO ENTHUSIASM. WHEN YOU HAVE A LOT OF ENERGY IT IS NATURAL TO WANT TO GET RID OF IT, BURN IT. YOU DO THIS BY GIVING IT TO YOUR PARTNER. GIVE. GIVE. GIVE.

PRINCIPLE #4
MAKE STATEMENTS

If you have the answer or are the answer to people's problems, there is no need for questions. Questions create doubt. Statements create power, e.g. *Am I the right person for the job?* as opposed to *I am the right person for the job* or *Is your problem not knowing what to do?* versus *Your problem is not knowing what to do* You become powerful with statements, an expert in the minds of others.

Dr. Martin Luther King's "I Have a Dream" speech wasn't riddled with questions. It was amassed with statements. It moved people to think. Common thinking tells us that questions insight thought, questions are thought provoking, but so are statements. Statements are definitive. They say something about you, your character, and your beliefs. We are attracted to people with common values and interests. We want people to stand for something.

Between three and five years old, our favorite question is 'Why'. It is a never-ending question. There is nothing less definite than 'Why'. I also know the inquisitive stage we go through in those years is rather annoying to those that have to answer the questions. That is why we have teachers.

Let's do a quick test. Consider you are in a business meeting with your client and your boss. Your business can be anything for this situation. Which one of the following do you feel is more powerful?

Where are we going to get that? or *I'll start making calls and figure out the best place to get that.* Put yourself in a boss' shoes first. They hired you because they believed you were capable of handling situations like the one you're in. They don't want to do your work. This is why you get paid. I know you might be thinking you don't want to make a bad decision, so you want your boss' input. Awesome. Tell your boss. Here is that statement: *I'd love for you to share any suggestions for the best place to get that.* Statement. You are submitting to your boss' power while still making it known that you are capable of completing the job without his input.

Asking a question in this situation also doesn't make you look good in front of your client. Your client hired you because you are going to get a job done for them. They hired you, not your boss. Making statements shows you are in control. Your client needs to know that you can handle the job you've been hired to do. You aren't making your boss look bad. You are making yourself look

48

good. You are showing that you are okay reaching out for help from someone who knows more.

Questions also put a lot of pressure on the person you are asking. If your boss doesn't have the answer in that instant, you've just made him look bad. That won't be good for you. If the scenario was just you and your boss, you still shouldn't ask the question. Make a firm statement and let your boss respond. *I found several places where we can get that.* Your boss' response may sound something like this: *Great, let me see them.* Another statement. He will let you know which one he thinks is best.

By making statements you control the moment. Once you start asking questions, you relinquish your power in a situation. Here is my last example: The police bring you in as a suspect of a crime. If they already know the information, why would they ask you any questions? In order to receive your confession, they just make statements. *We know you did it. We have several witnesses. We caught you red-handed.* Asking questions here reduces their power; it creates doubt. It shows they are unsure. *Where were you? Do you know several people saw you? What if we told you your prints were found at the scene?*

This goes for any situation in life. Questions create doubt. Statements create power. I'm assuming you want to be in a position of power because with success comes power. Use it wisely my friend.

PRINCIPLE #5
MAKE OBSERVATIONS

We are so busy thinking about ourselves, we fail to see the world around us. Take it in. Remember that we are here to serve a purpose and that purpose involves others. The problems of the world that resonate with you most often are the ones you are probably being called to solve. These problems create your purpose. You are here to solve these problems the best you can. I find the more observations I make, the more I learn. The more I learn, the easier it is to meet the people who will help me succeed at fulfilling my purpose.

We are so in tune with others and their energy, but we often fail to act on it. We don't want to invade people's space, their lives, we think if they want to share they will, but they won't. Fear stops them. If we make observations verbally about those around us, it forces people to live in the moment. It creates a connection.

Relationships fuel our lives. So by making observations, people feel connected to you. It just takes the one right connection to launch a career, start a family, or create a movement.

You can't see much but old gum, cigarette butts, trash, and shoes when you have your head down. Look people in the eye. Be a great audience member to the world.

You can only discover something by observing. You can learn just as much from observing as from doing. Watch someone throw a football. If you watch what they do, you'll learn how to throw. Of course the only way you will master it is by doing it, but observation is key.

There are multi-millionaires who have come up with inventions based strictly on observation. George de Mestral is a perfect example. If you don't know the name, it's okay. He only created a product that revolutionized fasteners. In 1941, after coming back from a hunting trip with his dog in the Alps, he removed some burdock burrs from his clothes and his dog's fur. He observed them under a microscope and quickly saw the burrs were hooked at the end. This drove him to invent what we know as Velcro. All he did was observe nature. It wasn't only his observation of the burdock burrs that led to the invention. He had to find a problem it would solve. It was stronger than tape, more lightweight than zippers; it could be used in infinite locations. The problem it solved wasn't found right away, it took numerous years. He basically came up with an invention of reverse order. He found a solution but didn't know the problem it was going to fix. That took a lot more observation. Most inventions are created because the inventor observes the problem first, like the light bulb, the phone, or the automobile. The problems these inventions solved were observed prior to the desire to create something. It was the problem that started the brainstorming.

ACTOR'S RECAP: BY MAKING OBSERVATIONS (WHICH ARE COMMONLY STATEMENTS – PRINCIPLE #4), YOU CONNECT WITH YOUR PARTNER. IT SHOWS YOU CARE (PRINCIPLE #1). BY SHOWING YOU CARE, IT STRENGTHENS YOUR RELATIONSHIP (PRINCIPLE #2). PAY ATTENTION TO HOW THESE ALL COINCIDE, ALL TEN OF THEM PLUS THE RULES.

PRINCIPLE #6
ADD INFORMATION & BE SPECIFIC

We tend to leave out a lot of information- men more than women. Women love details, but the problem is they normally aren't relevant.

Information is power. You are currently reading this book for that exact reason. If this book was comprised of just the following sentence: *Don't make life complicated,* that would be wonderful but that information although a little specific would be much more helpful if it told me how not to complicate life.

The reason most of us aren't specific when we add information is because we don't believe it is pertinent. Most people who lie will leave out a lot of details because they would have to remember them again. So they make things vague. If you are going to share, then share specifics, and I'll tell you why. I can't say it enough: a major contribution to our success is the relationship we have to others. When we talk about it's who you know, well, you really have to know them. You have to be willing to share specific information about yourself for them to share about themselves. It builds trust. Tell me whom would you trust more, a man who tells you he is married or a man that tells you he is married to a woman named Sarah. I'll give you a second to think about it. That was long enough. So, if you didn't say the man who tells you he is married to a woman named Sarah, you must have a thing against a Sarah.

When we omit information, when we aren't transparent, people tend not to trust us. I know you may want to call bullshit, but a lot of this happens subconsciously. In my experience, when people don't add specific information it means they are trying to hide something. I don't' trust someone who is hiding something.

Adding information and being specific lends itself to having even more opportunities of building a stronger relationship with people. It always amazes me how people feel they have a stronger connection to you because they are related to or know someone who has your name. That information becomes a topic of discussion, a point of relativity, a bond. That information can lead to even further seemingly arbitrary topics of discussion.

They aren't arbitrary though. These topics are meaningful to both parties. Remember our two basic needs in life, *love* and *acceptance*. Having a conversation with someone about hard water (a seemingly arbitrary topic) doesn't seem important or meaningful on the surface, but minds, hearts, and spirits are connecting on a subconscious level. We feel like we aren't alone in the world.

Adding information provides access to you. I grew up in Chicago, probably the best city I know (at the moment). I think of myself like Chicago. I'm lively, a little dangerous at times, culturally diverse, and open to everyone. So if I'm like Chicago, you must be thinking what information am I adding to make myself open and accessible? The answer is roads. We've heard of the information super highway. Well Chicago has added very specific information (roads) to get to it, to enjoy it, to grow with it. My information super highway is my words, whether written or spoken. I'm creating a road to me. If you have the right vehicle then you can get to me and guess what, everyone has the right vehicle because we are all human. Being human is the vehicle. You just have to make sure you take the roads specified to reach me (Chicago).

ACTOR'S RECAP: ADDING SPECIFIC INFORMATION PROVIDES DIFFERENT PATHS YOU CAN TAKE IN A SCENE. THE MORE PATHS ESTABLISHED THE GREATER THE OPPORTUNITY FOR A STRONG SCENE. THE INFORMATION SHOULD BE SPECIFIC TO RELATIONSHIPS TO PEOPLE, PLACES, AND THINGS.

PRINCIPLE #7
CHANGE DIRECTIONS

Obstacles are a part of life. We can't run through walls, but we can change direction. We can dig under it, go around it, or climb over it. Sometimes we may need to move laterally for a moment in order to overcome an obstacle. This doesn't mean that we have turned away from our goal. We are just finding another path to get there.

This is not just a physical reference but also, and more importantly, an emotional one. Emotions equate to action. When you *feel* your life needs to go in a different direction, you act on it. The most difficult part of this is we normally are so far into a rut that it is difficult to take action. Being ever present gives us insight into our current state. Being in the moment, practicing ImproviZENtion allows us to do this. The problem is we don't necessarily take action until our emotions are at an extreme. We take action when we are moved to take action. Anger causes us to punch people in the face. Happiness causes us to hug and kiss others. Frustration and criticism is a call to action.

The only constant in life is change and although we know it, we fight change. Yes, it is uncomfortable but greatness comes from those that change directions. Think about a firefighter. The firefighter changes their emotional direction when running into a fire. The natural, innate feeling is to run from a fire. The feeling is fear, but the firefighter moves into a different emotional state and that moves them physically into fires. That is why they stand out to us because they aren't on the street watching. They aren't part of the audience; they are part of the show. They are living in the moment not watching the moment.

The firefighter does not do this without training and practice. They train their minds to generate the opposite of what it is innate. You too will only be able to do this by training, practicing. Even when you have changed directions it will be uncomfortable. Think of Dr. Martin Luther King. He trained himself to embrace the people that despised him. It had to be uncomfortable. To go in the opposite direction of which you normally travel is always uncomfortable. The possibility of you getting lost and not knowing what that path will look like often keeps us from that change. Commit to the change. If it becomes too uncomfortable you can always change directions again and head down the path of familiarity, but it is normally when it is most uncomfortable that you are the closest to success. Being at the base of Mount Everest is much more comfortable than being at the summit.

ACTOR'S RECAP: OUR JOB AS ACTORS IS TO TAKE PEOPLE ON AN EMOTIONAL ROLLER COASTER, NOT A PLAIN, BORING TRAIN. THE BEST WAY TO DO THIS IS TO CHANGE YOUR EMOTIONAL DIRECTION. FIND A REASON TO HAVE A MOOD SWING.

PRINCIPLE #8

CONNECT TO YOUR PARTNER

Partner: a person who shares or is associated with another in some action or endeavor; and life is an endeavor. Life is action. So, we are all partners in life and the greatest connection we can make is through touch.

Actions speak louder than words remember? If I punch you in the face, not only have I told you I want to hurt you and that I'm angry, but also that you hurt me. That one simple action connects me to you instantly. That one simple action conveys one of the strongest emotions we feel. Our deepest feelings are always shown in silence. Realize our deepest feelings consist of love, fear, anger, and sorrow. These can be conveyed with touch and often should be. There is a Zen saying that states, Do not speak unless it improves upon the silence. I actually believe that words more often than not convolute interactions and relationships. The moments we feel the most are the ones when we are connected with someone else.

Let's talk about sex. This is not only a primal connection but also one of intimacy. It is the greatest connection there is because the basis of it is to create life. Now, that may not be what is going through your head when you are having sex, but realize that if sex was painful rather than pleasurable, humanity would die off. At the end of the day avoiding pain is greater than gaining pleasure. No matter how great the pleasure is, we would rather avoid the pain that we associate with it. Back to sex. The majority of people like to caress, cuddle with, or for the absolutely lazy, fall on their partner. Again, touch is extremely important here. Affection is the purest sign of love. Just think about the last time you had a fight with someone and they withdrew their affection, which by the way I think is a horrible tactic. I'm sure you didn't feel loved by them anymore.

Touch doesn't have to be that extreme. We don't have to have sex with everyone. Simple touch is just as moving. Think of a handshake. It's not that big of a deal, or is it? I'm sure someone has given you the limp-fish handshake. I know I've received several and I always make a point to ask why. That handshake definitely tells me something about the person, but how does it make me feel? I don't feel important, welcome, or appreciated. This handshake tells me that the person doesn't have any confidence in themselves and they don't care. PRINCIPLE #1 - CARE. It's that simple. If they don't care about themselves, I don't really want to care about them. They haven't put forth an effort to care about their handshake with others. If you are reading this and think that a handshake is not a big deal, you don't really want to connect with people and you are probably the person with the limp-fish handshake.

In order to move from it's not what you know to it's whom you know; this is a very important moment, the introduction. Anyone who is anyone has a great handshake or they hug people when they meet them.

I like going out to eat. I treat my servers like people not like servants. When I do this, they want to do more for me. They want my experience to be outstanding because I connect with them. I prefer to work for someone that values me as opposed to someone who could give a shit about me. They are thinking more about themselves. There was a company that has only eleven employees. In their first year of business, they were ridiculously successful, so much so that they gave each of their employees a million dollar Christmas bonus. You would think someone would have quit. No one did because they felt valued. We want to be where we are valued even if it means that we aren't paid as much.

ACTOR'S RECAP: TOUCH YOUR PARTNER (PHYSICALLY). IT CREATES AN INSTANT CONNECTION. POWERFUL CONNECTION EQUALS POWERFUL SCENE. IT'S EASIER TO BUILD A SCENE WHEN YOU FEEL VALUED.

PRINCIPLE #9
RAISE THE STAKES

When we don't get what we want, we justify not having it. It's very easy and common. We make excuses. The people that attain success do so because it fulfills a need, not a want. One really nice thing to have is a brand new car, the supposed "carcinogenic" new car smell, the handling, and the bells and whistles. They give us a sense of accomplishment. There are plenty of people that purchase or lease new cars, but let's talk about the people that want a new car and don't get it. The have a list of excuses:

-It's too expensive

-The insurance will be too much

-It's just going to get ruined by my children

Here is the thing: when your want becomes a need, you don't have any excuses. I've heard several highly successful people tell the story that they had no back up plan, no plan B. The reason is because if they failed to have one, they had to make sure they succeeded with plan A. It would be easier for them to come up with excuses to quit. You need to eat so you make sure it happens. You fight for it (this doesn't mean a fist-fight, but can). You do things you might not ever thought you would. You swallow your pride. You beg. You eat scraps and garbage. You don't do it because you want to; you do it because you need to, in order to survive, to live. It becomes a life and death situation. So if you were to make your want a need, you don't stop until you attain it. You fight until you have no more fight; you fight like there is something to lose.

There are things in our lives that when we lose them it feels like death, family, friends, and our dreams. Everything else that we lose, that makes us feel like a small piece of us has died, simply equate to the previous stated relationships. We suffer the most when we lose them. I want you to realize the relationship inanimate objects create or build. You may lose your phone and that may feel like death but that is because you are not able to contact friends and family. Inanimate objects have importance because of how they relate to our friends, family, and dreams.

I think smart phones are ridiculous. Sure, I like to have information in the palm of my hand, but let's face it. We have become more ignorant because of them. We can just look things up. We don't have to think. We don't have to process. With that said, a smart phone is a necessity in the acting industry. Actors receive last minute auditions. So I *needed* a smart phone that would get me my emails instantly. My smart phone equates to my success on some level; I need to succeed as an actor.

I've already addressed being needy. Needs are always met while wants can be justified if they aren't achieved. Needs are created when we view something that can be the difference between life and death. The only things we receive in life are our needs.

ACTOR'S RECAP: THE 'FIGHT' YOU GIVE IN ORDER TO OBTAIN YOUR GOAL IS IN DIRECT PROPORTION TO WHAT YOU WILL LOSE. IF YOU WILL LOSE YOUR LIFE, YOU WILL 'FIGHT' THE HARDEST. EQUATE ALL CHOICES TO LOSING FAMILY, FRIENDS, YOUR DREAMS, OR YOUR LIFE.

PRINCIPLE #10

LOCATION, LOCATION, LOCATION

If you don't know where you are, how will you know where you need to go to get what you are looking for? Location is very important in your life, professionally and personally. We aren't just talking about physical location. Where is your mind? Where is your heart? Where is your spirit? They all have to be in good, supportive, positive places.

Another saying that I've heard quite often is, *It's not where you are from, it's where you are at.* English majors are probably freaking out because the sentence ends in a preposition. The point of the saying is for you to take notice of how far you've come and to focus on the present. This could possibly create some challenges in your thinking. One could look at how far they have come and be proud of their growth while others will look at how far they have come and be disappointed. Either way, it gives a lot of insight into what needs to be done to move further along in your success. If you are happy with where you are then all you have to do is continue. As I previously stated, I grew up in a Chicago ghetto and moving into a better neighborhood not only became motivation to stay in a better neighborhood but made me realize there was better.

You can position yourself for success. You do this by working hard toward what you want and eventually what will happen is you happen to be in the right place at the right time. We call it luck, but there is no luck involved, even someone who wins the lottery. In order to win, you must play. Winning the lottery without playing, that would be luck. That would be a miracle but when you purchase a ticket, you are positioning yourself for success. What is the alternative? You don't purchase a ticket. In this instance you have not positioned yourself for success. I'm not saying to go out and purchase lottery tickets, but if you do, you actually have a chance of winning.

Whether you believe it's what you know or whom you know, you still must be in the right place to find either. If you want to be a lawyer, your location should be where you would gain the knowledge to be a lawyer, whether in a law school, a courtroom, a coffee shop where lawyers frequent, or in an apartment as a lawyer's roommate. It sounds a little silly, but logically it works.

Lastly, you need to really embrace your location. There is a reason you are where you are at the time you are there. Most of the time we have blinders on and move through life without taking in our environment. We miss opportunities because we fail to connect with our location. It may sound ridiculous but your location provides a lot of information about where you are and where you would like to be.

Do you eat at McDonald's? What types of people eat at McDonald's? Think about it. Rich and successful people don't frequent McDonald's, unless those people are the board of directors for the company. Rich and successful people have the money to spend on higher quality food, so they do. Sure, at this moment, you may not be able to afford to frequent these places, but know this location and others are the places you'll find yourself when you start up the ladder of success. If you find yourself there on occasion, here and there, you are telling the universe this is where you belong. If you continually find yourself in McDonald's instead, you are conversely telling the universe this is where you belong.

Make a choice to be in a location that will position you for success. Make your location meaningful. Your location leads to your *real* estate.

ACTOR'S RECAP: YOU NEED TO ESTABLISH YOUR LOCATION AS QUICKLY AS POSSIBLE BECAUSE YOU CAN ALWAYS REFERENCE IT. LOCATION IS HIGHLY IMPORTANT BECAUSE IT GIVES YOU A LOT OF INFORMATION WITH WHICH TO WORK.

POST-PRODUCTION

<u>CURTAIN CALL</u>

You're not finished. The most important action comes after the performance. See, once you are living an Oscar-worthy life, you have to give your acceptance speech. This is what it should include: First and most important, gratitude to those who have helped you along the way, then humbleness and humility, and lastly, words of encouragement and inspiration for those who are taking the same path.

We aren't successful without the support of our clients, customers, fans. It is their recognition that creates our success. It is by helping others that we become successful. We are simply here to serve others. Your life has no meaning without others.

I promised you would know the meaning of life by the end of this book. Here it is.

THE MEANING OF LIFE
IS TO GIVE MEANING TO OTHERS' LIVES.

You are here to serve others; educate others; love others. Your purpose is to be what other people need you to be, a brother, a sister, a father, a mother, a giver, a receiver, a comforter, an obstacle, a motivator, an example. Be the best you and give thanks for the opportunity you were given to touch lives, change lives, and create lives.

NOTE:

To know and not to do is the same as not to know Learning takes immersion. If you've only read the information once, you will most likely not retain the majority of it. Read this again and again and apply the information daily. This will guarantee you see, feel, and are the change you desire.

PRICELESS PROSTITUTE

Soothing bath
You wash me
Paying special attention to my privates

Drying me off
Powdering me up
Rubbing me down

You take me to your bed
Comforting me
from my reoccurring nightmare

Loneliness

Placing my head on your bosom
Caressing my hair

You offer me your womb
I crawl up inside
and for the night
I am saved

What a small price to pay

Bibliography

Thoreau, Henry D. "A Quote by Henry David Thoreau." *Goodreads.*
Goodreads, 10 Jan. 2007. Web. 28 Nov. 2014.
<http://www.goodreads.com/quotes/2690-i-went-to-the-woods-because-i-wished-to-live>.

Made in the USA
Charleston, SC
03 February 2016